SOULED-OUT ENTREPRENEURSHIP

THE 4 EVERS TO BEING ICONIC.

DR. ROLLAN ROBERTS II

Courageous!

WHERE AMAZING HAPPENS.

Published January 2019 by Courageous! Media & Dr. Rollan Roberts II.

INTRODUCTION.

In the age of never-stop-working, sleep-when-you're-dead philosophy of success with total obsession, money dominates, and lavish life-styles, many are left empty. The high-priced motivation and hype can be valuable for those that are stuck in life and business and for those just getting started on their entrepreneurship journey. It's good starter milk.

But the more successful you become, the emptier it will leave you. Their audience usually stays obsessed with them and this content for 2-3 years until they outgrow it. I experienced this firsthand from age 19-21. And it left me on a perpetual journey thereafter trying to dis-cover the deeper principles of the fulness of joy and success. This book will take you from sold-out to souled-out. You will work less, pro-duce more, experience significance, gain influence, create legacy, and have better health, better relationships, and a depth of peace that you don't think is genuine or possible right now. You will have everything that money cannot buy and the money to buy the things it can.

This book will take you from sold-out to SOULED-OUT.

The prevailing "Pinterest Success Philosophy" of our day gets it par-tially right. You do have to be obsessed. You do have to be focused. You do have to work hard. You do have to forsake things. You do have to be intentional. But that's just the beginning; it's breastmilk. And yet, it is being presented as the beginning and the end. You're still hungry because it's not enough. It's not the full meal.

Souled-Out Entrepreneurship unveils the deepest inner truths of the successful entrepreneur. It's the truths that the gurus always come to after making it big hyping the milk lifestyle. I know because they con-fide in me after this runs its course. I sat with the king of no-money-down real estate informercials in the 90's, and he had taken a 3-year sabbatical around the world, in monasteries, and searching every relig-ion trying to discover what I share with you over the next few pages.

Go deeper. Give up the philosophy that you've clung to that has got-ten you the success others told you was the pinnacle. There's more. So much more. And you know there is because you feel it deep in your spirit. Grow past "doing" and enter the significance of "being." Discover how the 4 Evers open up the deep, rich rivers of Souled-Out Entrepreneurship.

DR. ROBERTS WITH WORLD LEADERS AT DIPLOMATIC ROUNDTABLE IN BEIJING, CHINA.

1

THE HEART OF SOUL.

Entrepreneurship is the single, greatest, global economic force in the world. Once considered outcasts and unemployable, entrepreneurs are the modern-day rock stars. We tame lions and slay giants for breakfast, and that's just the beginning of our day. But we are starting to see the risks of entrepreneurship with a divorce rate of 91% among entrepreneurs – failed marriages, failed health, failed families, failed faith.

There are deep emotional challenges because of the massive loss, betrayal, and pain it takes to be a successful entrepreneur. That is what sold-out gave us - superficial, artificial, temporary financial success with brokenness in areas that matter most.

And while being sold-out is part of it, who and what you're sold out to determines if you are Souled-Out. And the essence of the blissful, peaceful success most people imagine is only achieved by being Souled-Out. People consist of three parts – body, soul, and spirit. You are a spirit; you have a soul, and you live in a body.

The soul consists of your mind, will, and emotions. People can afflict, destroy, and kill your body. People can afflict and destroy your soul (mind, will, and emotions). People cannot touch your spirit.

Your spirit is more than your intuition or gut instinct. It's significantly more than that, and reducing your spirit to intuition is doing yourself a great injustice and tremendous insult, if not blasphemous, to your spirit. Leading from the heart is really leading from the spirit. The heart is an organ. The spirit is the eternal part of you that guides your destiny.

In order of importance, your spirit comes first. Most people focus on working out and controlling their mind and thoughts by thinking and being positive. I'm telling you straight up that you absolutely cannot achieve real success by focusing on the body and soul alone, or even first. You can achieve what looks like the real thing, the outward trappings, but you will be empty and not understand why. You will be out of alignment. You will not be consistent because the right behaviors of body and soul emanate from the having the right spirit.

People who take shortcuts in losing weight eventually gain everything back plus a lot more. We can praise the weight loss, but time shows us how it was achieved by if it is maintained or not. Time always exposes those who take shortcuts to success as well. So please do not start with the soul and body. Settle the destination of your eternal spirit first.

Once your spirit is settled, and assuming it has chosen the right path, you will spend a lifetime converting and keeping your mind, will, and emotions in alignment with the right spirit because it is not natural. Things that are destructive to our soul are what comes naturally – fear, worry, doubt, resentment, revenge, bitterness, and anger – all of which cause illness and disease in the body, such as arthritis, indigestion, diabetes, and more.

Your success is largely determined by how you control your soul.

Your physical health, financial status, relationships, and overall success is largely determined by how you control your mind, will, and emotions. Most people do not control these at all and let them be whatever they wish to naturally be. They let their emotions are the deciding factor, and if you haven't been deciding, I can guess what it has predominantly been doing for you.

Souled-Out Entrepreneurs must discipline their minds. You must discipline your mind to dwell for long periods of time in silence on objectives that you seek without your mind wandering to what you don't have or what you think you need.

The conscious mind is very tactical in that it creates lists and plays the devil's advocate on everything. It's generally negative, not realistic. One problem may be you think realism and being realistic is what you can see. That's short sighted and completely ignorant. You can't even see what is real because the realist thing in the world is the thing that lasts, and that's your spirit, which you cannot see. You do not live in the spirit realm, you live in the physical realm, and the physical realm is only one dimension of the real realm! What you refer to as real is simply circumstances, and if you haven't noticed, circumstances change quickly.

> **The focus is "being" not "doing."**

Joseph spent thirteen years in a pit, as a slave, and in a jail, and in a single day was promoted to second in command in Egypt when it was a world empire. That career path doesn't make sense. That defies the logical mind. That defies the "real" world. But it does not defy the eternal spirit world. Your previous businesses have failed because you didn't get this, challenged it, denied it, or wouldn't study it! You too, will go from the pit, to servitude, and to a prison before ending up in a palace once you understand Souled-Out Entrepreneurship.

Years (not minutes, hours, days, weeks, or months) of pouring, not trickling, the right input into your conscious and subconscious mind is what it takes to get your mind in its entirety programmed correctly. I address some of the most critical inputs directly throughout the book, but know that who you call friends, the people you spend time with (whether voluntarily or involuntary, such as coworkers), the people you choose to follow on social media, TV, radio, the books, articles, and magazines you read are all forms of input. And they're dangerous. They all present a worldview that you have been accepting or rejecting.

You must ruthlessly evaluate and cut people, things, and inputs from your life that are not in alignment with eternal truth. Notice I did not say "your version of truth." Your version may or may not be eternal truth. It may be circumstantially and factually accurate, but that

The will is an extremely powerful tool when it is directed in full and complete alignment with your thoughts. That is why it has been said that it's better to be hot or cold than lukewarm. All good or all bad is better than half-good or half-bad. Be all of one or the other or you will lose at life. One leg in with one leg out is the recipe for disaster, whether in business, relationships, or life. You will fail in every sense of the word by doing that.

<u>Emotions</u>

The third part of your soul is your emotions. Nothing better describes the age in which we live better than this. We live in the Emotional Age. Everything is about how you feel. Everything is about doing what makes you happy. Happiness is heralded as the pinnacle of human achievement. How destructive, empty, and false.

We live in emoji-filled worlds that illustrate if we are happy, sad, angry, depressed, laughing, laughing hysterically, or confused. There are emojis for emotions I did not know I had. We are constantly asked to describe and express how we feel.

> The goal isn't to change how you feel; it is to change how you think. Emotions serve as a high-level feedback mechanism for right and wrong thoughts.

Allow me to burst your feelings bubble. How you feel should be completely irrelevant to you. Tired? Sad? Broke? Discouraged? Hurt? Excited? Euphoric? It is important to recognize the emotion, but it only serves you to the extent it allows you to know what kind of thoughts you should be thinking next. If you have a negative emotion, you must forcefully change your thoughts. Your soul will fight your spirit on this, but if you will change your thoughts, your feelings and emotions will follow. You see, your feelings aren't very smart. They are easily tricked, fooled, and manipulated (remember this the next time you want to quit your life, marriage, or any good thing!).

It is fine and healthy for those that love you to be concerned with how you feel, but you should not be concerned with how you feel. How you feel should only serve as a feedback mechanism and window into how you are thinking. Your feelings will never align with your destiny. They will never take you where you want to go. They serve one purpose and that is as the gauge of your thoughts. Master your mind and thoughts because those control your emotions.

This puts a hole in the self-care movement, but the principles I'm sharing to be a Souled-Out Entrepreneur is the greatest self-care program you could ever enroll in! You do not have to control your emotions. Control your mind and thoughts, and your emotions will control themselves. Right input equals right output.

One of the greatest challenges of leading a company daily is controlling how you respond to the incessant onslaught of problems, challenges, complaints, and crisis. If you lived by your emotions, like the vast majority of people do, you will be exhausted by 11am and be completely worthless and ineffective by the afternoon. You will have anxiety attacks, nervous breakdowns, mental crazy spells, digestive problems, and heart attacks. Do not try to change the emotion or feeling for emotion's sake. The goal isn't to change how you feel; it is to change how you think. Emotions serve as a high-level feedback mechanism for right and wrong thoughts. Feelings are not the ultimate guide to your inner being. They are very surface level that provide immediate feedback. It may even be inaccurate feedback. That is where your mind must evaluate if that feeling comes from a place of truth in your spirit and right thinking.

For example, drug, alcohol, and sex addicts may feel pretty good and happy for a period of time. Their emotions may tell them they are happy, in love, and having the time of their life - because emotions lie, deceive, and are easily manipulated. But when those emotions are evaluated from spirit truth and your right mind of what's healthy and right in those conditions, one quickly realizes that they were fooled and deceived. And the longer they stay engaged in such behavior, the harder it is to get out. The harder it becomes to change your thoughts, rewire your brain, exercise your act of will, or control your behavior. You succumb to being reduced to a child that is subject to and controlled by every whim of emotion. And so your life and business decisions are in a constant state of simmering turmoil.

Pain is a wonderful gift if it is used properly. It's destructive and disastrous if not.

I have worked with people like this who get so frustrated because even when they did the right thing, they weren't getting the right results. It's because these people tried to change and conform to the exterior and refused to work on the interior. They cared about the façade but rebelled against this philosophy on the inside. That creates what has been defined as a double mind. And double minded people are unstable in everything they do, even when they do the right thing, because they are doing and their being isn't aligned with that action. You cannot fake this. I've seen the best deceivers on the planet try, and they exploded and imploded within a year of trying to fake this 24/7.

We have been taught to avoid pain at all cost. But loss and failure creates pain. Loss of finances, loss of a job, loss of a spouse, and a thousand other smaller losses create pain after pain. Pain is an emotion. It is not until we learn how to use pain as fuel that we stop being victimized by it. Pain is a wonderful gift if it is used properly. It's destructive and disastrous if not.

As an entrepreneur, you will feel pain like few people will ever understand. You will be betrayed, slandered, mocked, abused, broke, stressed, exhausted, and at heightened inflection points of failure multiple times. You will experience the full spectrum of financial, relationship, and business problems that most people experience over the course of twenty years in three months. These evoke strong, negative emotions out of most people and thus the cycle of traditional sold-out entrepreneurship filled with divorce, financial loss, poor health, and fractured relationships continues. You do not need sold-out; you need Souled-Out.

You might have been expecting me to give you marketing strategies, aggressive lead generation techniques, and the ultimate tactical guide of daily disciplines that keep you in sold-out entrepreneur beast mode. And I would, except I've already done that - along with every other author that experienced a level of success that society applauded. And the conclusion that most come to after that season runs its course is how fleeting and temporary that behavior and mindset is. The more worthwhile journey is pursuing spirit then soul because it creates the solid foundation from which every kind of success imaginable emanates.

As an entrepreneur, your soul influences every single decision you make, and you're making hundreds of them a day. Your business isn't having a financial problem; you are having a soul problem. The problem isn't your product recall; it is your soul. You don't have a culture problem; you have a soul problem. Fix the soul, and you fix the problem.

Incidentally, you do not have a marriage problem, you have a soul problem. You do not have an addiction problem, you have a soul problem. Unless you have age-appropriate ailments, your physical problems may be soul problems.

There is no greater work of life than thought. Therefore, it should be your highest priority as a leader.

How much time every day do you dedicate to mastering your mind and flooding it with the right input? Most people are so busy that this is an afterthought, if even a thought at all. Yet, this is the true work of life. It is the highest form of work you will ever engage in. And your success is directly proportionate to your attention to it. There's a difference in elevation between those who give it thirty minutes and those who give it three hours.

DR. ROBERTS' FATHER TAKING OATH AFTER WINNING WEST VIRGINIA STATE SENATE.
WV Legislative Photography, Photo by Will Price

2

FINDING CALLING IN CAREER.

The last thing you want to do is give your all to a company, project, or cause that is empty. Oftentimes, we have skill sets that can be applied in many different ways. Accountants can account in virtually every industry. Leaders can lead in most any setting. So how do you know your ladder is leaning against the right wall? How can you know that you are applying your efforts in the right place at the right time and in the right way?

It starts with understanding your purpose on earth – knowing why you are here. My life has a single mission and purpose here. It doesn't change with age; it doesn't change with vocations or roles, and it does not change based on who I meet. In fact, my very identity is rooted in this purpose.

You are more than what you do. You are more than the title on your business card says you are. Average people do not understand this. That's why middle and upper managers often go into a state of depression after losing a job or experiencing a loss that they deemed important – be it a charitable board position or president of the home owner's association – whatever title or role they wrapped their identity in.

The same thing happens to professional athletes when they retire. They knew who they were as an athlete, but who are they now that they aren't doing what they've always known? Executives often wrap themselves in the brand of their company. When they no longer have that brand behind them, they act different and have a completely different demeanor. That's a case of mistaken identity. The most successful people in the world aren't trying to be, they just are. They know who they are, and why they are here.

To find your calling, you must first understand your purpose, and that is only possible by understanding who you are. This is not a five-minute conversation with yourself because the answer to this ongoing internal dialogue will change your life. It changes who you can spend time with. It alters your daily schedule. It will establish what is acceptable and not acceptable in your life. The aspects and details of life flow from the outcome of the identity you've consciously or subconsciously chosen to assume. If you've chosen correctly, it will never change. Just like the ultimate purpose of your existence does not change. This serves as the firm foundation on which you can build a life worth living and experience success worth having.

Your calling is what changes. How you execute your life's purpose and identity will evolve and change over time. It will be different in various seasons of life. I don't have to be called to a company to work for them. Sometimes, I just needed income so I did what I had to do. My purpose didn't change, and I wasn't called to serve or make a difference in the work, it was simply a stop gap. I don't only do the things I'm called to do. You will not achieve what you desire if that's your approach. Success will require you do many things you don't want to do, or would rather not do, in the pursuit of your calling and the fulfillment of your purpose.

As you walk in your purpose and identity, there will be defining moments in your life – callings – where you know that, regardless of the outcome and results, it is what you are meant to do. It is your destiny. That, my friend, is your calling. Walk in it. Own it. Abandon what others will think of you. When you step into your calling, society's metrics of success are irrelevant. How much money you make doesn't matter. It might cost you everything you have. You may sleep in your car for months like I did. But you know you are right smack in the middle of your calling, singing the music inside you, being guided to a higher level that conventional thinking cannot take you. Everyone else may look and see tragic circumstances, but you are confidently walking in your calling. Your circumstances haven't caught up to the calling you are walking in. Those around you will not understand, for it is not for them to know, which is why what they think cannot matter.

Now you understand why I am not called to serve every client I have or every activity I engage in. When you are called, it is always for a task bigger than you. It is outside of your existing skill and will require you to rise (change and grow) to the occasion.

Ultimately, you do not find your calling as the chapter title suggests. It finds you. You simply walk in faithful diligence in what seems to be mundane work doing what you know you are supposed to do, fulfilling your purpose, and walking in your identity, then WHAM – it comes along. Maybe you recognize it immediately, and maybe you don't, but you will recognize it as it unfolds.

> When you step into your calling, society's metrics of success are irrelevant.

If you are waiting on your next assignment, the key is constantly keeping yourself in the right state of mind and being that is ready to accept your next calling. The longer you are made to wait, the more you are being worked on and developed. The refining and pruning process takes time. Elevation takes time. And what may take years to germinate can grow exponentially in unrealistic and unforeseen timeframes.

Waiting is hard. Successful people like being busy. It makes us feel productive. But it is highly inefficient and unproductive (despite how many things you're checking off a list). Waiting pushes us to finally succumb to doing something to keep from going mad or it molds us into a level of peace, calm, mental discipline, and internal fortitude rarely seen in the world today. Waiting causes many to distract themselves with entertainment, noise, vices, and wrong entanglements. In case you didn't fully hear it, waiting right (without distracting yourself with people and things) is the hardest work you will ever do. It will drive you past the point of complete madness to a sphere of deeper understanding and wisdom that equip you for your next calling. Waiting right is the preparation for your next assignment.

If your assignment is worth anything at all, it is going to exhaust you. It will require every ounce of energy you have and leave you depleted somewhere on the journey. That is simply what happens when you lose yourself in your calling. You have to be rested up to be sold out in every part of your soul. The longer you wait, the bigger the mission, and the more you need your rest. Rest disproportionately to what seems normal in the waiting. If you are busy, tired, distracted, and exhausted, you will not have the strength to dominate your calling.

Waiting gives you time to heal. The longer you're forced to wait, the more whole you are becoming.

You have to be, and keep being, long after you think things should have already happened for you. That's what is making you who you are. That is what's preparing you to completely embody your next assignment. You may step into the role of a great leader, but you will not be filling their shoes. You will redefine the very space of what it means to lead in that environment. It cannot be compared because you have been uniquely prepared in the dark, in the unknown, behind-the-scenes for this stage at this time. You have stepped into your calling that no one else can fill. No one else can be you. They can (will) imitate. They can (will) hate. They can (will) resent. They can (will) duplicate. But they cannot be you. If all you focus on is what you do, you'll be like everyone else. And others will be better at it than you. Rather, focus all of your effort and attention to being who you are supposed to be so that when you step into your calling, you aren't a phony. You are not a fraud; you are the real thing.

DR. ROBERTS WITH THE FOUNDER OF EFAX AND OTHER GLOBAL COMPANIES AT GLOBAL ECONOMIC FORUM.

3

THE GIFT OF PAIN.

One of the hardest parts of surrendering to the first ever – Whatever – is that you have to accept, embrace, and even find joy in pain. That pain may be physical if you are an athlete, but in most cases, it will present itself as deep loss of….well, everything – family, friends, finances, possessions, things you cannot even think of. And there isn't a rhyme or reason to it that we can see, other than the pain will ultimately find what you value most. It must in order to create enough pain in your life to change you. We all have a pain tolerance to loss in areas of our life, but what about when you are stripped of absolutely everything? If your identity isn't firm, you will actually believe you've been stripped of the very essence of who you are. This is the darkroom that builds champions and creates leaders.

All great leaders train in obscurity. Joseph trained for leading Egypt in a pit and a prison. David trained for the kingship of Israel as a farm boy. The actions and behaviors of winners do not depend on whether the boss is watching, scouts are watching, or the spotlight is on. They do the right thing when no one is watching because of who it makes them, not for what others may think.

Pain positions you. It puts you in places you must be to catapult into great destiny – on your face and at the very end of yourself where you cannot go on. The greater the pain, the greater the possibility for greatness. Little pain equals little greatness. It's when you went through what would make everyone else alive bitter and when you take the excruciating pain that left many a person by the wayside that molds and forges you into a Souled-Out Entrepreneur.

Pain positions you.

All I want to know about a person is how he responds to pain. Who are you when you are in the throes of deep, dark pain? How much pain can you tolerate before you flip out? How little does it take before you become vindictive, resentful, or bitter? What does it take for you to walk out and quit? Your wins do not tell me anything about you, or what you are made of, but your wounds and scars and pain are what makes me trust you. It is the very thing you are taught to hide and run from that makes you trustworthy at all.

Those you lead aren't interested in your highlight reel. They follow you because of the pain you went through and came out a better person. You did not pile junk upon junk and hurt upon hurt. You went through trial after trial and became purer in the process, not more worn out and bitter because you knew your purpose. You knew who you are and have the right identity, and you did not distract yourself or numb the pain in the waiting. And mastering your soul, mind, will, and emotions during that time when it is the hardest to do is what healed you. It wasn't the spa days, beach vacations, and massages that healed your pain. It was waiting like a winner in the pain. It was having the right mindset towards the pain. It was consciously choosing to embrace the house of pain rather than the house of pleasure, entertainment, and distraction.

Not only is personal pain the best teacher in life, it is a requirement of greatness. No one has ever achieved the pinnacles of accomplishment without it. Even Jesus Christ himself had to endure massive pain equal to the massive success. Resurrection power only came from resurrection stillness.

Pain shows what you are made of. Society tells you to get over pain by distracting yourself. Your friends want you to go out, hook up, get out there, go places, and do things. Therein lies the deception. The odds of you ever healing from that pain is drastically reduced when you do that. The numbness starts to feel like healing, but it will surface down the road at your next job, in your next business, or in your next relationship.

The goal of pain is not to see how fast you can get over it. The only way to make pain work for you and turn pain into gain is to feel it. Feel every last bit of it. And decide with an act of the will, guided by your spirit, and bringing your thoughts into captivity and under the spirit's subjection (because they're going to be all over the place!) how you will process the pain and the greatness that it is producing in your life. The difference between isolation and solitude is your attitude and behavior in the waiting. It is how you are thinking about the pain. If you are thinking negatively and destructively with thoughts of anger, bitterness, resentment, and confusion, you will be isolated and depressed. If you are processing and understanding how the pain is shaping you into a greater calling and destiny, then you are in solitude that produces joy, peace, and contentment.

That is how you sleep in the midst of life's most volatile storms. That is how you have so much peace that the raging storms of life do not phase you one bit.

I am not telling you how to achieve greatness for one month or one year in business or life. I'm laying out how to make winning a part of the very fabric of who you are. It becomes a part of your DNA. That's how you have 50-year marriages. This is generational Souled-Out Entrepreneurship.

No eternal achiever ever said, "I just want to be happy." That's what people who perpetually chase happiness say. They chase it in people. The seek it in jobs. They pursue it in pleasure. The height of their joy and happiness is when their favorite sports team wins or they get what they want. That's the lowest form of happiness and is the shortest imitation of happiness that exists.

Perpetual bliss and happiness is a by-product of embracing pain. Happiness is found in the contentment that comes from waiting appropriately and indefinitely. You become generally happy all the time. There may be moments of inflected happiness, but that is usually manifested in a heightened sense of gratitude. You are flooded with thankfulness for absolutely everything in your life.

Pursuing happiness is one of the emptiest feelings one can have. Pursuing peace in all its forms, however, will reap dividends now and forever. Stop pursuing happiness. Start pursuing peace. You will think clearer, have brighter ideas, and make better decisions.

4

WELCOME TO CLASS.

One of the great paradoxes of Souled-Out Entrepreneurship, is that you cannot be tied to the outcome. That is counter-intuitive to our goal-driven culture, but it is not the way of highly successful people. Souled-Out Entrepreneurship is attached to disciplined thinking and behavior that places far greater value on the process long after you could have "made" something happen.

I have great vision and know where I'd like things to be. I also know that what will happen is much greater than anything I can imagine if I refuse to force, manipulate, or control outcomes. I know you can make goals happen. You even put dates on it and write it down. Congratulations, you're done with day one of Kindergarten. We have to move far beyond that to get where you are destined to go.

I made the mistake of living by this "Success Principle 101" of goal setting for years. It never fulfilled. In fact, it often created many problems. It certainly had me focusing on the wrong thing, and that misdirected focus created fallout and a steep price for the results I did not want to pay. That is not the price of success; that is the price of focusing on the wrong priorities.

You will get better results without the consequences of traditional goal setting when your exclusive focus is on thinking the right thoughts every single moment of every single day for every single year and simply being who you ought to be in the precise circumstances you find yourself, while trying to improve them. You must be dedicated and consistent to the right process, right thinking, right philosophy, and right decisions of the will (and all the wonderful emotions and feelings this way of living offers).

I have gone places and achieved things that no goal setting plan could have ever taken me. There's not a path to that sphere of accomplishment. What if I was too distracted by achieving one of my previously narrow-minded goals (like being the

> **Goal setting that focuses on outcome instead of process and behavior is exactly what was getting me off course.**

CEO of a billion-dollar company)? What if I was so insanely focused and sold-out on achieving some resolution I had set for my career or finances? I would have viewed what has become my destiny as a distraction. The very thing I desired, that I could not have even imagined, could only blossom when I got out of my own way. And goal setting that focuses on outcome instead of process and behavior is exactly what was getting me off course. Traditional goal setting is focused on the result, but the value, growth, and fulness of destiny is found in being not doing.

Being souled-out allows you to be open to opportunities you did not know existed and would not have even known to set as a goal, much less have the foresight to get there. And if it is a pinnacle no one has ever achieved, you do not know how to get there. Sure, you have ideas on how to get there, but you do not know. The only way to get where no one has ever been is by focusing on the process and always being. That is the only way. You see this in the life of all the greats, whether from thousands of years ago or those in our age. Many times, it looked like they were done, finished. Then years later, they come, what seems like, roaring back. Truth is, they never stopped being. We see the ups and downs and make judgements based on that, but when you focus on being instead of outcome, what appears to be setbacks do not slow you down.

Losing everything is not a setback. It's the next logical step on a journey that produces greatness. It's necessary to lose everything, and continue losing everything over and over again, until you can lose everything and stay souled-out. That is, losing everything and continuing to have the right spirit, control your thoughts, will, and emotions under the most intense set of circumstances humanly imaginable. The worse the circumstances, the better it prepares you. We have viewed and misunderstood the rules of nature, life, and success all wrong, and that is why more people do not live their best life. They may be living their dream life, but they sure aren't living their best life.

Once you dwell in this space, you are open to the first Ever of Souled-Out Entrepreneurship - Whatever – whatever action you are supposed to take, whatever step you're being shown, whether it makes sense or not, whatever word should be spoken, whatever song is to be sung, whatever skill you should pursue. You have finally arrived at the place where you're willing to do the right whatever.

I'm sure you were already willing to do whatever it takes to achieve your goals and dreams without doing all of this prior work. However, it would have been the wrong whatever. You would have been climbing the wrong ladder and wasting years getting to where you thought you wanted to be (how many career, interest, hobby, and business changes have you had so far?). Being willing to do whatever it takes is the old-school, ineffective, sold-out model of success and personal development. Most are willing to do whatever it takes as long as it is something they have to do, not be. Doing is easy. Being is hard. Doing whatever it takes will keep you busy and running around feeling productive, but you'll run in circles and eventually tire out. The Souled-Out Entrepreneurship model accomplishes more by attempting less. I'm less interested in your willingness to DO whatever it takes and more interested if you're willing to BE what it takes.

You may have told yourself for years that you're willing to do whatever it takes to win, but you haven't given up your way of doing things. There's too much ego. Your drive and ambition get in your way every time you power through. You haven't been willing to do

> I'm less interested in your willingness to DO whatever it takes and more interested if you're willing to BE what it takes.

whatever because whatever requires you to abandon a certain sense of self. In many re-
gards, whatever strips you of your dignity. It strips you bare to a level of nakedness where
you'll wish it was only physical nakedness. You're exposed. You're vulnerable. It is in
that whatever space that leaders are born and champions are made, whether they be
seven or seventy-years old.

5

RULES ABOUT NICHES.

I try not to shake my head when virgin entrepreneurs tell me their bright idea and will not seek or listen to counsel. Ideas are one thing. Execution, and who should implement them, is another.

There are a lot of conflicting truths and paradoxes in the world of entrepreneurship. And opposing strategies, philosophies, and tactics can all be right in a certain industry, with a certain product line, in a certain economy, in a specific geographic area, in a unique target market, or any infinite combination of these and other factors. Price point is a major consideration, along with the product category and target market (not the one you choose, but the one that chooses you). What is extremely valuable today may be completely worthless tomorrow. Market conditions change rapidly. Technology and the various adoption or rejection speeds of advancing technology all influence the success of seemingly unrelated products and services. World events have an impact. The variables are simply too many for you to waltz in with your pretty PowerPoint business plan and bullheaded approach to launching the next big thing.

You've got to be a whatever Souled-Out Entrepreneur because the whatever will always be changing. The right approach may be something you have never heard of or does not currently exist. That's why you've got to be a focused whatever entrepreneur! That's how you end up being in the right place at the right time. And if you're souled-out, you'll be doing the right thing as well! If you're only sold out, you'll be stubbornly following your business plan without regard for anyone or anything else and be in the right place at the wrong time or the wrong place at the right time. It is the epitome of self-centeredness and selfishness and ends with your demise.

> ## Niche the audience, not the product.

The market you are targeting has to be large enough to get you where you want to go (with only capturing a small percentage of it), yet narrow enough for your messaging and unique value proposition to be heard, felt, and experienced. The holy grail of target marketing is when you can have a single, focused message and a focused product or service mix that appeals to various communities of people. It allows you and the company to stay focused, but your messaging resonates with and is adaptable to multiple brotherhoods.

And I recommend targeting tribes and groups, not data elements. Instead of choosing a target market the way digital ads and direct mail make you choose your target audience by age, gender, location, net worth, pets, kids, career, title, and thousands of other data points with numerous deciles (decile one most closely aligns with your target up to decile twenty that's a far reach from your ideal client but not totally out of the realm of possibility), niche with close-knit ideological groups. The Golden Rule of Niching that virtually every entrepreneur gets wrong - niche the audience, not the product.

This requires significant discipline. Most entrepreneurs start sold out to their product or idea, but without first being souled-out, they do not have the discipline to do this. It is too tempting to accept every opportunity that comes along or chase every incremental revenue rabbit that pops up. It is natural to tailor your product and service to a niche constantly harping on how your widget meets the unique needs of that market without effectively speaking to the right community. Or worse, you speak to numerous tribes of people trying to connect with them all out of the gate. Apple communicated with graphic designers. That was their core. They never marketed to business executives, but they won them. They never targeted soccer moms, but they attracted them. When they did market to a new tribe, it was students.

There's not a wrong target group to select, but the one you go after will dictate the size and scope of your possible growth. You have to align your expectations to the maximum revenue objectives, time frames, cost of entry, lifestyle (it's a full-time strategy as in 24/7/ 365). A tribe of one hundred coin collectors will result in limited sales if that's the extent of your efforts compared to one hundred billionaires or world leaders in the room. You're working with the same number of people, but an entirely different audience which results in different revenue-generating expectations and time it will take to penetrate that audience.

By the time you figure all this out, the market has, or is about to, change. You only keep up and move to ushering in the next big thing when you are a Souled-Out Entrepreneur. It's being, not doing. It's being, not faking. It's being, not copying. It's truly being that resonates from your spirit and is evident in every thought, will, decision, and emotion. Now you understand why entrepreneurs like this are heralded as rock stars and superheroes. It is an extremely rare club where no amount of money can buy membership. It is who you are not what you have.

P.S. That infuriates most people! They are so used to being able to make it happen, force things, will things into existence, and manipulate to get what they want, but they aren't welcome around Souled-Out Entrepreneurs. Not because of what they don't have or haven't achieved, but because their spirit and soul are not aligned. People know their own kind, just like species, and you can automatically tell who belongs (because they are and have been), and those with disingenuous motives and bad actors (being kind and not calling them frauds). Those with a kind heart often believe in people like this anyway hoping that if they taste the genuine, that they'll long for it. That would be a rare exception of epic proportions. I do believe in miracles, but it took many years and a lot of pain to realize I'm not the miracle-worker. Be selective and spirit-led by who you mentor and coach for this very reason.

DR. ROBERTS AWARD IN TIANANMEN SQUARE, BEIJING, CHINA FOR HIS WORK ON THE US-CHINA TRADE WAR.

6

SOULED-OUT ACHIEVEMENT.

Souled-Out Entrepreneurs rarely celebrate their accomplishments. They recognize and acknowledge them but realize it's merely the result of everything else. The spirit and soul should be celebrated every minute of every day for that's what created that result. Most people worship the achievement (the graduation, the sale, the election, the position, the job, the outcome), but Souled-Out Entrepreneurs know that the main thing to be celebrated is the person they had to become to achieve it. That's why souled-out leaders don't celebrate cars, houses, planes, boats, and things. Those are irrelevant to your past, present, and future. Take it all away, and they're the same person. Take it all away from someone that is not souled out and see what happens! You've never witnessed such falls from grace, destruction, nastiness, meanness, bitterness, and anger. That's because it was or had become their identity, and when they lost it, they lost their identity. They weren't souled-out.

It is unnecessary for me to expound on how Souled-Out Entrepreneurs handle achievement, for once you are souled-out, it comes quite naturally. Sharing the dynamics that you can see simply helps the imposters know how to better fool more people. While it is unnecessary to teach, it will add value for the Souled-Out Entrepreneur to evaluate where they are and potentially refine their mind, will, and emotions before, during, and after great achievement.

Do not celebrate choice in the trivial matters of life.

What you have done or what you have accomplished is not what defines a Souled-Out Entrepreneur. Achievement in the souled-out world is not based on performance. Achievement is the result, but that is not what gets celebrated. The real accomplishment is being who you're supposed to be the other 364 days of the year. It's the early mornings, late nights, the times you did it when you didn't feel like doing it, the times it was inconvenient, the times when every fiber of your being wanted to do anything, but that was the real accomplishment. That was the quiet achievement that no one will ever see or know but you. And that's what matters. That is why the Souled-Out Entrepreneur handles the outward achievement with grace and celebration, but not with a frantic, absurd excitement. Look at how Olympians handle winning gold medals. They know the result of that one performance was a reflection of their achievement, not the accomplishment itself. They had already been that before the rest of the world saw the scoreboard in that moment. They were long before the result was made known to the rest of the world.

Success is not performance-based. It is being-based. Being is not a performance; it is a state of being. How many hours, days, weeks, months, and years can you think right, control your will, master your emotions, and surrender to the right spirit? Staying in that space regardless of the circumstances, regardless of the problems, regardless of the trials, fires, floods, financial losses, job losses, and relationship losses is the very essence and embodiment of success! It is a skill that very few have developed, and that is why it is the most admired and respected success one can achieve. It usually results in money and power, but money and power isn't the accomplishment – it's the byproduct of being in this space for a prolonged period of time – months, years, decades, a lifetime – because it's actually who you are.

Achievement, and the constant pursuit of pleasure, do not coincide. It is small minds that need to be constantly entertained. Every day could be a Disney day for them, and it still isn't enough. It amazes me how people who work long hours at work want to spend their time off at theme parks, escape rooms, sports, and anything that is considered entertainment that they can do (not experience – do). They have to be busier when they aren't working to escape their reality. Without realizing it, they plan so much to keep their mind busy. But why? What buried hurt or pain are they running from? What are they trying to distract themselves from? Achievers think the exact opposite of this. While they enjoy these pleasures with the right people (4th Ever - Whoever) on occasion, it is an afterthought, not something that is overly looked forward to.

Choice elimination is one strategy of Souled-Out Entrepreneurs. Sold-out entrepreneurship tells us there are unlimited options, when they are actually unlimited distractions.

I limit my decision making to the absolutely critical things of life. I do not want to dwell on the mundane. I automate daily decisions – what I eat, where, drive, routes I take, and every repetitive decision I can. Those will eat up your life and keep you from meditating, listening, and dwelling on significant accomplishments and the strategies and ideas to get there.

I'm not actually having to look over menus at restaurants to choose what I'm going to eat. They will have a very small handful of options that conform to how I eat, or I'll order something custom. I'm not standing in front of the closet daily deciding what to wear. I have standard looks and clothes that can be mixed and matched for casual, dressy, or formal occasions. I simply do not want to spend valuable thinking time on important, but trivial, matters that should be automated. But if that is the biggest accomplishment in your life, then I get why that's what you focus on. I'm helping you understand why you don't accomplish anything of global significance – because you can't get there doing what you're doing, thinking what you're thinking, and being who you're being. Hating or despising those who do doesn't change what you're going to do this weekend or on your next vacation.

Do not celebrate choice in the trivial matters of life. The narrower the options in that category, the more clarity you will have in areas of significant. Those are the areas most people do not have time to think about because they're trying to figure out the fastest route to work, what to eat for lunch, what entertainment they're going to do after work, who they're going to invite for a drink, what they're doing this weekend, and how they're going to spend their next vacation. What an empty way to live. So much choice, and all of it on things of meaningless value.

DR. ROBERTS ADDRESSED CHINA'S COMMUNIST GOVERNMENT AND
BUSINESS LEADERS IN THE GREAT HALL OF THE PEOPLE IN
TIANANMEN SQUARE ON THE U.S.-CHINA TRADE WAR.

7

GEOGRAPHY MATTERS.

It took me years to get to where I was being and reflecting the first Ever – Whatever. And I
thought that part of being and doing whatever meant I was willing to go wherever – until it
is no longer theoretical, and you have the choice that will completely change your life as
you know it. You have to lose friends, lose family, lose the familiarity, lose the dining and
shopping conveniences, lose your place of worship, lose relationships, and literally walk
away from everything that gives you stability in the physical world. And you have to
decide now.

Unless you have been there, you still cannot fathom what that moment is like. I've had
several of them and have only adamantly moved forward three times. What makes the
second ever – Wherever – so difficult is that you are making a tremendous sacrifice

without knowing, or being guaranteed, a desired outcome. If you were offered luxury accommodations, full provision, meaningful work, and position, it would not be a difficult decision. Professionals make this decision every day when their jobs offer relocations that come with pay raises and promotions.

That is not what I'm talking about for Souled-Out Entrepreneurs going Wherever. I was reminded of this truth recently when I was in talks with the board of directors from a large, household-name organization that wanted me to be their CEO. I really liked the idea, love the organization, and could see a path for leading them into a strong growth future.

As the talks became more serious, I started looking for property near the corporate office. It was in a small suburb of a larger town in a part of the country that I have absolutely no desire to live in. I recognized this principle warring within myself a I was willing to do Whatever but really struggled with the Wherever.

It struck me how ironic it was that I was willing to do Whatever, but not Wherever. I was being sold-out, but not souled-out. Furthermore, I was willing to spend weeks in China, but wrestling over a move in the United States. It would have been an easier decision if I was moving out of the country as opposed to a place I did not want to be domestically.

If you're like me, you may initially think that going and being wherever is part of whatever. And intellectually, I still grapple with this. But when you are faced with it, you experience the stark difference between them. My mind recalls the famed preacher of old who loved what he did. He was completely sold-out! And then he was told to go preach to an extremely controversial people group. If he went, he would lose a lot of prestige and notoriety that he had gained. He would lose positions of prominence. He would be slandered and falsely accused. But he knew he couldn't stay where he was after being told to go, so he did leave, but went to a more desirable location. He convinced himself that because he was still doing Whatever, the Wherever didn't matter.

Wherever Souled-out Entrepreneurs have reached another level of success. For you will not be presented with this decision when it is logical or easy. You will be presented with it when you have everything to lose. You will be confronted with this decision when it is illogical, frightening, risky, and not popular. This goes way beyond simply moving (which is still ranked in the top three most stressful life experiences). The act of moving is easy. Being led to the right place at the right time for the right reason is another matter entirely.

Geography is important. Starting where you are is important. You can start "being" in a cubicle, prison cell, or the White House. You can be digging a ditch, working a mall kiosk, or running a company and start being right where you are. In fact, there is no other way to start being than to start being immediately right where you are.

There's no waiting for a new week, month, year, career change, relationship change, financial change, or geographic change. You start being right where you are right now. That's the way of the Souled-Out Entrepreneur.

To finish the story of the preacher, the ship he was on almost wrecked in a mighty storm. He knew the only way everyone would escape with their lives is if he was off the boat (attempted suicide). His fellow travelers made that happen, and Jonah spent three days in complete isolation before surrendering to the Wherever. How long does it take you to decide to do the right thing when you will likely lose everything you have worked for your entirely life? These are the moments that let you know if you are sold-out or souled-out.

It is easy to rationalize why geography doesn't matter. In this age of technology, is it still as important?

It is to sport teams. It is to politics. It is to companies. Does a professional athlete's talent improve by going to a new team? No. But the variables of coaching, other players, culture, attitude, and environment can elevate them to win a championship with one team that they could not with another. A politician can win in one city, state, or country, and lose in all of the others because geography matters.

Location, as I speak of it in the Wherever context, is not a data-driven decision. It is spirit-led. That is why you occasionally hear about people taking pay cuts and demotions. They are following their path and not conventional wisdom of success to constantly move upward. Constant upward movement is a myth that keeps you playing too safe to really win big. The most successful people in the world and the history of time experienced a measure of success, then great failure, followed by greater success than before, and more failure. It seems to vacillate between these extremes until they enter a place of ultimate stability and prominence (think Abraham Lincoln, Joseph, Moses, and David).

> We are promised to reap what we sow, not where we sow.

Ask any of these examples the role geography played in their success. It was everything. But they could not shortcut the process. They had to follow a geographic path and be in places they knew they were not destined to stay in. They had to be a Wherever Souled-Out Entrepreneur to know where they ought to be and when, whether it's where they wanted to be or not.

What further complicates this for so many people is that, often, you aren't just deciding for yourself. Maybe your spouse is completely against a move to the great unknown. Perhaps your kids are thriving in their current school and environment. Without fully jumping to the fourth Ever, this is why who you choose as your life's mate is critical. It is so much more than love - or happiness (don't even get me started again). You have to be aligned. If your purpose is fully aligned, achieving your greatness and destiny is a million times easier. It actually makes it possible. When you're married, it's not enough for you to be souled-out; your spouse needs to be as well to achieve unparalleled greatness or you will have to choose between souled-out or marriage. It will likely be chosen for you since you'll try to do both as it will either physically kill you or your partner will leave.

Industries

I took the same job title, the same job functions, and the same skill set from a large company to a small company and more than tripled my salary. I had been doing the right thing at the right time in the wrong place.

Margins vary tremendously by industry, and so does your quality of life based on which industry you choose to be in. If you choose (hopefully you don't let it choose you) a low-margin industry, you will forever be living under ridiculous cost controls and a scarcity mentality. I don't do well in those environments. I thrive in limited-resource environments, just not in scarcity-mentality cultures – and there's a huge difference between the two!

Examine the lifestyles, cultures, and decision-making infrastructure of various industries to decide where you operate best from. Career coaches have had this wrong forever. They are so focused on helping you find the right vocation or position, but they have failed people in that all positions are not created equally. Being a police officer in Mayberry is very different than a police officer in Los Angeles. An accountant for a local fast food restaurant has a very different life, experience, and pay than an accountant for a public auditing firm. You may be doing the right thing at the right time just in the wrong place or for the wrong industry.

Titles

One of the challenges would-be Souled-Out Entrepreneurs struggle with is how they will be perceived or what their title will be in the new land. They are very concerned with image. Your social or financial status cannot have any bearing on whether or not you will surrender to the Wherever of Souled-Out Entrepreneurship. Titles are important for the masses to understand roles and responsibilities, but the leader is perfectly fine without them. I do not need to be introduced as the CEO of this company or on the Board of that organization to have influence or identity. My identity is not in a position that I hold or a responsibility I have. That is what I do, not who I am.

I am appropriately aware of perception and image as we are instructed to be. This is not suggesting you be something that you are not; rather, it is that we are cognizant of staying away from the very appearance of wrongdoing. Wall Street recently charged all males along these lines in how they interact with females when they laid out rules of engagement that would avoid the appearance of wrongdoing in the wake of the #metoo movement. This is not a debate of right and wrong, rather, it is an awareness of perception, which leaders should be cognizant of, but not concerned by.

Pop culture tells us to have an "I don't care what anyone else thinks" mentality. This is heresy, selfishness, and self-centeredness (which they promote) at its worst. You are not a god, nor are you perfect. So until you are, it would behoove us to consider how our words and actions make those around us think and feel. Only miserable people live for themselves. Happy people give and serve without expecting anything from the receiver in return. They fully expect a life of abundance, merely not at the hands of the receiver. We are promised to reap what we sow, not where we sow.

Titles are a part of the fabric of our global society. All Militaries have ranks and titles. Every company and organization have titles that give structure, power, and authority to various levels accordingly. We become consumed with titles and take them on as our identity because they are so heavily revered by society. They carry immediate respect in many cases, and that is gratifying to self and to getting things done.

But the Souled-Out Entrepreneur must forsake this earthly system of hierarchy. You have to be equally at peace and contentment with joy and thanksgiving working in the dark in a garage and with the same hope, belief, determination, and authority you had when you were the CEO. Hardly one in a hundred million could ever do this. The mental discipline it takes to do this can only come from addressing, not numbing, the deepest, darkest pain imaginable and letting it forge you with an iron inner will and resolve that is kind, understanding, persistent, and perpetually clear on the mission.

That's why getting the title you want can be one of the worst things that happens to a person if they aren't ready. If they haven't been through the fires, floods, and trials that mold and fashion a person of highest character and integrity and responded properly during and after (this is the distinguishing factor as everyone is messy in their own way), they are not ready. They will crash and burn, and it is better for them and their mental sanity if they had never achieved it in the first place. The trappings of success have catastrophic mental effects on people that are not ready.

When you surrender to the second Ever – Wherever, you forfeit the right to understand why that is the place. You may not understand, but you must accept. One can never get to this state of being without having mastered the mind, will, and emotions. The uncertainty is too great, coupled with facts that are contrary to what society has assumed is good counsel, and horrific circumstances that defy all odds for most people to think clearly, act intelligently, maintain a calm inner spirit, and discipline every thought.

DR. ROLLAN ROBERTS AT LIBERTY UNIVERSITY.

8

THE DEEPEST TRUTH.

One of the deepest understandings of life is an understanding of time. I'm not even close to staying in this space at all times, but I desire to be. I direct my thoughts, will, and emotions in this way, and it is in complete alignment with my spirit. Like everything else we have covered, the spirit economy of time has very different rules than we have inherently learned and by which the world must operate. There is the process and structure of time – seconds, minutes, hours, days, weeks, months, and years, and then there is a different sphere of time that is not confined or defined by these metrics.

Sold-out entrepreneurs, and most people, will only ever know the physical realm of time. That's all their brain is interested in understanding, and they even pay that very little mind. They are careless with their seconds, minutes, hours, and days so to think that there would be any interest in going deeper in understanding and having a more meaningful and impactful life is ludicrous. They can keep their entertainment, pleasures, and distractions. Souled-Out Entrepreneurs reap all the peace, joy, contentment, success, health, and fulness of life itself that comes by living in the actual spirit realm of time while operating in the physical constraints of time.

Both realms of time are necessary. We need the structure of units of time in ways that help us have a more developed and civilized global society. It is an effective way to communicate, collaborate, and harmoniously work together and accomplish things. We have many examples about the power of morning and evening routines. The physical element of time should be studied thoroughly, and good habits established as a result. There are many great resources on this subject, but time management is not the highest resolve. Living in the spirit realm of time is the pinnacle of living your best life.

With this understanding, we come to third Ever of the Souled-Out Entrepreneur – Whenever. It is one of the hardest of the four Evers to live in. I can operate in it one minute and be out of it the next because the spirit and physical realms of time compete with each other. They both want to dominate your life. And both in isolation will destroy you. Live solely in the spirit realm of time, and you are irrelevant. Live solely in the physical realm of time, and you are average at best. That is why I say – live in the spirit realm of time and operate in the physical realm.

> ## Live in the spirit realm of time and operate in the physical realm.

Have you ever been disappointed that something did not happen when you thought it would or should? I cannot even begin to tell you how monumentally disappointed I have been when things did not pan out the way I thought they should when I thought they would. I was willing to wait up to a certain point. And then there's the dumb success philosophy of make it happen. Right, let me know how the deal you forced, the relationship you made happen, and anything else forced works out for you. In most cases, force is illegal because it is a violation of someone else's will. And every time we violate spirit time, we have just violated ourselves. We just acted against the very thing that can help us if we work with it not against it.

Since spirit time does not have structure, it is based on more factors than science understands. Here is what we know – that while we wait, things are happening. Our level of belief or doubt contributes to what the result of our waiting will be. Our attitude, temperament, and words influence it.

Waiting seems to be the greatest of all hallmarks in spirit time. And it will intentionally take you well past the point you think something should have happened. And it heavily weighs how you wait to determine how often and to what degree you will be forced to repeat the circumstance. It may throw you a health problem, or a financial crisis, or a marital melt-down to see if and how you wait.

What you do in the waiting requires more mental and emotional discipline that any other thing you will ever encounter. To rightly handle hours, days, weeks, months, and years of waiting changes a person in the most profound ways that words cannot describe except to say, you will never be the same. You will be better. You gain wisdom when waiting intentionally in spirit time. You gain knowledge and understanding. You see things differently.

So if waiting patiently, calmly, and indefinitely is the main essence of living in spirit time, and how we wait is the main teacher that develops, refines, and refreshes us in the process, it is essential to understand how to wait. I don't know about you, but no one has ever taught me how to wait. We have been told to wait, but not been taught how to wait. Patiently, yes, but that's hardly scratching the surface. It almost does not even belong in the conversation because it is such a distraction to how we should wait in a manner that brings us through and leaves us better than before.

Waiting used to drain me. The longer an unresolved financial or relationship problem dragged on, the more stressed I would become. The less faith I would have. The more hope I lost. The more physically weak I became. The more mentally exhausted I was. All this because I did not know how to wait. I could have experienced great joy in the great times of trial that seemed to drag on and on. I could have experienced some of the deepest peace man has ever known during that time because that is the times you can best experience it.

With waiting being one of the most noble manifestations that great things are happening in the spirit realm of time, Souled-Out Entrepreneurs must learn to not get in the way and mess things up, which we seem to be excellent at doing.

We must not wait in fear or worry about the future or how our present circumstance will be sorted out. We must not be consumed with anticipation of a certain outcome. We should wait in expectation and complete belief that the process is purifying and burning off the rubbish in our lives and will produce, in our waiting and stillness, a better outcome than we can see in the midst of turmoil. Perhaps not the desired outcome, but a better one no doubt.

With all of the forces of time and competing forces for your energy and attention, being still is one of your greatest weapons. Stillness is the single, best thing you can be and do while you wait. And part of stillness is being willing to wait indefinitely. Waiting with the right thoughts. Waiting with the right emotions. Waiting with the right behavior. Waiting with the right outlook and energy. You do not wait for a certain period of time, you wait until. That is souled-out thinking.

It is easy to hope for the best when you're busy, active, or distracted. I remember in a great season of waiting and stillness wanting to walk around, go places, and do things –

My spirit and soul can be still while my body is busy.

simple things, benign things, and perfectly healthy things. But I knew that pull was to distract me from the work of being still and knowing. I naturally wanted to be active and know, be busy and know, be distracted and know. It would be easier for me to know if I didn't have to fully acknowledge the full set of circumstances and could know it would work out, then distract myself with nature or friends to lessen the pain of the process.

If I had indulged at that time, I would have been running away instead of letting the process do in me what it was trying to. When someone is discouraged or depressed, people always try to get them out of the house. Some of the most common advice I hear people give to hurting people is to keep their mind busy (distracted). Yes, do that if you want to repeat that circumstance over and over the rest of your life. Or you can fully feel the hurt and pain and properly grieve and grow from it for however many hours, days, weeks, months, or years you need to so it doesn't rear its ugly head in a future relationship or endeavor.

Sold-out thinking acknowledges the power of timing – when to act and when to wait. But it has nothing to say about how to wait. We are not educated, nor is there curriculum, on operating in the physical realm of time while living in the spirit realm of waiting and stillness.

My spirit and soul can be still while my body is busy. And it must be to accomplish greatness. It is living the purest form of life, while looking like a paradox with opposing truths and realities on the surface. That is why it took me years to get to this place of being. But getting there is worth the time, work, and effort. It is a prerequisite for elevation and greatness. That is why my reality can be different than what others see, because my mind is operating in a spirit realm of time and my body in the physical. Physical time always lags spirit time.

I reservedly use such a trite illustration, but by the time my books get published, I have accomplished so many other things that I usually have to go back to read what I wrote. It was my reality long before it was anyone else's. It is also why overnight success takes at least ten years. You can be suppressed, oppressed, and rejected for years, but by waiting in stillness, you develop an uncanny strength and determination that kept you going, kept you improving, kept you producing, and kept your mind and heart where it should be, then one day you get the call. One seemingly random day, your talent or skill is noticed, and you are immediately elevated. Athletes experience this when they get signed to professional teams or receive major endorsements. Actors experience this truth when they star in the first major role. We see it in politics, corporations, and society.

Ascension takes time, and then the exaltation happens suddenly. David knew he was next in line as King of Israel while he was still tending sheep for sixteen years. And he was forced to wait and be still even knowing his final destiny. He did not start moving into the middle management ranks or start grooming for the position to run the country like we would prepare in the physical realm of time. And this illustrates how much we do not understand about how greatness is created. It happens in isolation. It happens in the dark. It happens in loneliness. It happens in pain. It happens in betrayal. It happens in financial loss. It happens in the worst times of life where we joyfully wait, and sing, and praise, and give thanks in absolute stunning silence and stillness.

And the longer we wait, the more we are being prepared for even greater things. Trivial accomplishments need minimal preparation. Great accomplishments require great preparation.

You will experience no greater test in life than being still once you know. The tendency of great leaders is to act, fix, and make it happen since you know that is the destiny. And doing so will delay your expectation even longer. Joseph knew his destiny and so began thirteen years of abuse, slavery, and literal imprisonment for something he didn't do. And then he became Vice President of Egypt. Moses waited forty years. Jacob waited fourteen years. Even Jesus waited eighteen years. But you want it right now. You think you have paid your dues. You think you've earned it. Because it's all about you and what you want and when you want it. That attitude shows just how much more waiting you desperately need in complete stillness and surrender to spirit time.

People fail at life because they keep trying to make it happen instead of wait in stillness. They try to find a mate through desperate measures instead of waiting and being. They try to accumulate wealth by investing things they have to learned and waited. They simply do not understand, nor operate by, the highest truth of time. Just because you are still doesn't mean nothing is happening. It means more is happening because you settled down. We have such high opinions of ourselves that things can't get done or won't get done right if we don't do it. We demonstrate so much arrogance when we do not wait.

It does all work out like it's supposed to when you surrender to this truth. It does not work out like it's supposed to for those that don't adhere. Society has accepted a sub-par reality instead of choosing the souled-out path.

We see and experience the evidence of this with very few understanding it or how to intentionally create it. That is when I started enjoying and embracing the waiting seasons of life. I realized they were giving me much-needed reprieve to strengthen my heart and health while renewing my mind. It was designed to alleviate pressure and stress on me, not produce more. Rejoice in the waiting. Relish the stillness. Be intentional about the stillness and only do things and be around those that contribute to that stillness.

The interesting thing about the stillness is the answers you get to various problems, past or present, that you may be experiencing, along with ideas for the future. This is so much more than meditation. Meditation is an act; it is still something you do, and I am talking about something you be. It is not something you be from this time to that time, it is something you simply are. And those operating exclusively in the physical realm of time will push you like crazy because it drives them crazy that you aren't as stressed as they are about time.

Being still in the midst of an extremely hectic schedule with the pressing demands of leadership is the art of Souled-Out Entrepreneurship. Perhaps there is no greater attribute of the Souled-Out Entrepreneur than their ability to wait, be still, and do so with the right spirit, thoughts, emotions, and outlook. These are the kind of people I respect and seek counsel from. These are the rare ones that truly live, not just experience, life.

You have to choose your philosophy of time to live by or the default is naturally the physical realm. Live in the spirit realm of time and operate in the physical realm.

DR. ROLLAN ROBERTS WITH CHINESE DIPLOMATS

9

ATTRACTION.

The 4 Evers to Souled-Out Entrepreneurship – Whatever, Wherever, Whenever, and Whoever. The order is arranged in the way life taught these lessons to me. I started off sold-out. But it's not hard to be sold-out when you don't have much, or you do not have everything in your life to lose. Then you finally submit to the Wherever of life. Once you've been through Whatever and Wherever, life has a way of introducing you to Whenever. And once you live in the surrendered spirit realm of time filled with joyful waiting and rejuvenating stillness and peace, while operating in the physical units of time, there is only one more thing that can bring you down. There is only one more thing that can destroy everything you've built.

It is not a recession or depression. It is not physical illness, the stock market going down, or real estate values tanking. The fourth Ever that brings you down or lifts you up is the Whoever.

You never escape it. People will enter your life at eight and eighty. And this Ever will be the source of your greatest pain, hurt, financial loss, emotional loss, betrayal, slander, lies, and deceit imaginable. Because you have the right foundation and life philosophy that starts with the right spirit, and you have mastered your mind, will, and emotions for Whatever, Wherever, and Whenever, it makes it much easier to appropriately respond to the Whoever's that are not souled-out.

Kings that have conquered kingdoms have been brought down by a single person. Thrones have been overturned by a single traitor. Marriages are ruined by a who, never a what. Fortune 100 businesses crumble quickly because of the wrong who. Every good thing you have ever done, accumulated, or earned can be undone by a single, momentarily lapse in judgement with the wrong person. Hardly a day goes by we do not read headlines of politicians and leaders who are at the peak of their contribution and performance and a Whoever brings them down. Their accomplishments in the world are not enough to survive their character flaws.

> Every good thing you have ever done, accumulated, or earned can be undone by a single, momentarily lapse in judgement with the wrong person.

There is no greater area of life that we must be more diligent in than who we surround ourselves with. A person can be brought to nothing as a result of the wrong association, relationship, or friendship.

There are two critical truths that must be accepted in order to protect yourself from Whoever. Debating them is a complete waste of time as these are natural laws of human nature. First, you attract who you are not who you want. Second, who you let around you will determine the fate of your health, finances, marriage, relationships, faith, and success.

Honest people won't work for (or live with) liars. A players won't work for B managers. Our ancestors taught that birds of a feather flock together. At the beginning of each new school year, kids find their own within hours. So as mad as it might make you, you attract who you are not what you want. Tired of attracting the wrong kind of man or woman? Tired of attracting incompetent people in your business? Tired of being surrounded by "yes" people or deadbeats? The problem is more than the energy you're putting off. It's more than a vibe.

Companies and societies judge leaders by their spouses. That's because it tells you so much about a person. Who they chose and who chose them shows their level of emotional maturity, mental stability, and intellectual prowess. Your life's mate is the second greatest Whoever decision you will ever make in life (the first being your spirit choice). They will make you or break you. They will elevate you, destroy you, or render you useless.

I would love to spout off the ridiculousness we hear today about us being our own person and maintaining our singleness in marriage, but that's not how marriage was designed nor is that how life is meant to be lived. That may be an emotionally safe way of doing it, but it is not the souled-out way. That is sold-out thinking, and sold-out thinking gets sold-out results (stress, worry, anxiety, depression, divorce).

If you are attracting the wrong people, it is usually because one of two issues – one, maybe you like who you are and aren't willing to change, and two, maybe you have tried to attract the right people, and they haven't been attracted to you, and you are struggling to find your place and your people.

The first is just arrogant. You are attracting the wrong type person so you blame the person instead of the darkness within you that entices them. You're attracting the wrong type employees and blame the employees instead of the culture that attracts them and repels the employees you wish you had. The second is a tough place to be and definitely something I struggled with.

Much of the struggle comes because of time conflict. People can only observe and evaluate a potential friend or association through the lens of what they can physically see. The physical units of time may not have caught up to where you actually are in spirit time (your circumstances may not represent your actual state of mind). Simply scroll through someone's social media account to see what I mean. You can be totally in love with a person or think you just hired the greatest person in the world, then scroll through and scratch your head wondering why they would associate with people like that or engage in such unseemly behavior.

Don't scratch your head and don't wonder – that is who they were and may still be. Who people enjoy being around will tell you more about a person than interviewing them for a straight week. People can and will say absolutely anything to get what they want. That is why you have to look past words and actions and observe patterns, behaviors, and associations. Good apples never make bad apples good, but bad apples make good apples bad every time they are around them.

It's not enough to be an amazing person. Amazing people have done things they never, absolutely never, would have done after meeting or allowing the wrong people to be anywhere near their world. Former king of Israel, David, had a son that was next in line for the throne. After years of privately thinking about sexual fantasies with his half-sister, he told a friend of his how attracted he was to her. His friend told him he was the prince and could have anything and anyone he wanted. He even gave him the plan of how to do take her!

Sure enough, the heir to the Israeli throne followed the plan his friend said and ended up raping his half-sister. He was murdered by her brother shortly thereafter and lost the throne and life itself. The prince did something he never thought he would do, and never would have on his own – but he had a wrong friend. He had a wrong association.

And you will do things you never thought you would do, perhaps swore you would never do, if you do not viciously and ferociously guard, defend, and protect who you associate with.

People can get you to go places you ordinary would not go or where there is no need for you to be. They can get you to stay when you should go and get you to go when you should stay. The downfall of many, otherwise great, leaders has been this very thing. They stayed when they should have gone or left when they should have stayed (business trip, conference, family, obligations) and it created the environment or allowed themselves to be in an environment where things are known to happen. This always imposes a danger that requires additional caution.

You have to routinely evaluate where those people are that have your ear - it's not a "once you're in, you're in" mob mentality. People change because of wrong influences and associations, and you must constantly observe and discern who those around you are letting into their lives. They may let the wrong influence in their life at some point, and you have to recognize how that can and will affect you personally and professionally.

That is why it can be hard to associate with the right people because the right people won't just let you waltz in and be all chummy like the schmuck at the bar will. It takes time to observe people. And don't even start screaming about not judging people. There is a huge difference between observing and evaluating people and judging them. Judging them would be casting a right or wrong judgement on their actions, behavior, or person. Observing and evaluating is discerning if that person will be a constructive influence in my life by being fully aligned with my spirit and soul.

> **There is no greater area of life that we must be more diligent in than who we surround ourselves with.**

Discernment is the main skill to mastering the Whoever's in life. If you have already mastered the Whatever, Wherever, and Whenever, I promise you have more discernment than most. It may be learning to trust that instinct.

For me, I fully love, and I fully trust, so I have to be extra careful who I let close because I will believe in them and love them to my own demise. This is not a theory; I unwittingly tested it! I honed my skill of discernment in business but chose to ignore it in other areas of life. I still had it. I still sensed when things were off. And I did not respond and apply the discernment how I did in the areas of life where I was successful.

Most of the people in your life, you did not choose. Therein lies the answer to why you are where you are. It is why you may feel stuck, tired, or uninspired. You are likely surrounded by people who want to be but aren't being. There is nothing more draining than this. It will exhaust you. But how can you choose who you are around when you cannot control everyone your company hires or those in your department? You may not be able to control who your customers are so it forces you to work with people you may not otherwise associate with. Unless you buy up the street, you do not control who moves in next door. You do not control who attends your place of worship. Many of those around us have some level of input that we do not control or have influence over.

But why worry about those, when you haven't been worried or discerning about those that are closest to you - the ones you know aren't good for you and still refuse to immediately change. People are starting to celebrate the friends they get drunk with, those they get in trouble with, or those that always give them the wrong advice. You don't celebrate people like that; you run from them. That's not judging what they choose to do or what they think; it's simply choosing if you want that for yourself. Do not walk away - run. Immediately. Do not hesitate. This one action is the only thing that can save and protect everything you have built. No amount of insurance can equal discernment and responding with the appropriate action, no matter how painful in the short term.

The deepest pain I have ever known in my life was still short term compared to the big picture. I'm still enjoying the benefits of that pain to this day. But very few people are willing to examine, then root out, wrong influences and associations. It feels disloyal. It is contrary to our nature, but you learn to love the person without associating with the person. The relationship must be redefined as they truly leave you when they allow wrong influences and associations into their life. You haven't left them. You stayed the course. They got distracted. They became disillusioned and invited and accepted the inferior into their lives that will cause destruction for them and those close to them.

The wrong association has brought down the mightiest of people this world has ever known, and you are not exempt. No matter your success, no matter your title, no matter your wealth, and no matter your power, the wrong Whoever can absolutely destroy and decimate your entire life. You aren't souled-out until discernment and separation of associations and influences in your life happen subconsciously, consistently, and without debate.

Why the 4 Evers of Souled-Out Entrepreneurship? Because there isn't a category for who you are and what you are supposed to be. You're special. You are different. You aren't like everyone else. You have to do Whatever, Wherever, Whenever, and with Whoever in complete alignment with your spirit and soul, and in so doing, you will create and define a life that has never been lived before. Sold-out will leave you tired and empty. Souled-out will energize and empower you with side effects that bring great pleasure, joy, and happiness while creating generational legacy and blessing.

This is Souled-Out Entrepreneurship.

SOULED-OUT ENTREPRENEURSHIP

Entrepreneurship is the single, greatest, global economic trend force in the world. Once considered outcasts and unemployable, entrepreneurs are the modern-day rock stars. We tame lions and slay giants for breakfast, and that's just the beginning of our day. But we are starting to see the risks of entrepreneurship with a divorce rate of 90% among entrepreneurs – failed marriages, failed health, failed families, failed faith. There are deep emotional challenges because of the massive loss, betrayal, and pain it takes to be a successful entrepreneur.

That's what being "sold-out" gets you. Let me introduce you to what being "souled-out" gets you. If you've tried sold-out, and it hung you out to dry, Souled-Out Entrepreneurship will fill your soul.

Business success simply cannot be retained without being a Souled-Out Entrepreneur. Dr. Rollan Roberts gives you the "4 Evers to Being Iconic" as an entrepreneur. Whether you have a home business while working a full-time job or you are running a company doing a hundred million dollars, Dr. Rollan Roberts shares The 4 Evers of Souled-Out Entrepreneurship that directly address the deepest and ugliest parts of entrepreneurs to go through less loss, pain, betrayal, and crisis by moving from sold-out to souled-out.

www.SouledOutEntrepreneurs.com

Dr. Rollan Roberts II is the CEO of Courageous! Entrepreneurship, an advisor to world governments, the host of iHeartRadio's only national business call-in show, Courageous! Entrepreneur Radio, and former CEO of the Hoverboard company - the single, hottest, global, consumer product of 2015. In addition to being nominated to the Central Command Task Force for the Department of Defense, and keynote speaker at Harvard University and for Bloomberg, he has led several global, high growth companies and has a record of creating some of the fastest growing viral brands in the world. He has a Doctorate degree in Global Business and Entrepreneurship, founded the CEO Entrepreneur Cruise, authored 4 international best-selling books, and spoke to China's government and business leaders on the US-China Trade War at the Great Hall of the People in Tiananmen Square, Beijing, China.